Anointing
Christ's Healing Touch

by
Fr Jerome Bertram

*All booklets are published thanks to the
generous support of the members of the
Catholic Truth Society*

CATHOLIC TRUTH SOCIETY
PUBLISHERS TO THE HOLY SEE

Contents

Introduction 3

1. The Incarnate Word: Healing of the Whole Person 4
   Healing the wounds of sin and separation 6
   Miracles as Signs..8

2. A Sacrament from the Beginning of the Church............10
   The Church Fathers and the Sacrament of Anointing 12
   Scholastic Theology of the Sacraments.............................15
   Agreement and Disagreement 17
   Post-Tridentine Developments 19
   Recent Times...20

3. The Rite of Anointing the Sick 23
   The Old Rite of Extreme Unction 23
   The New Rite...26
   Public Celebration of the Rite 27
   Private Celebration 28
   In a Hospital Ward..30
   In Emergency...33
   Theology of the Sacrament 34
   Changes in the new Rite 35
   Form and Matter 38

4. Visible Effects of the Sacrament 42
   Remarkable Effects 43
   Healing the whole Person 46
   Those who do not recover 49
   Physical Healing 51

Further Reading 54

INTRODUCTION

Jesus went from place to place in Galilee, healing the sick, casting out devils, cleansing lepers, and raising the dead: when He chose His apostles, He gave them the command to do exactly the same, and so they did. The ministry of healing has never been absent from the Church, and at all times the successors of the Apostles have had the power and the duty of continuing the healing work of Our Saviour. For this purpose a special Sacrament was instituted, and it remains one of the regular duties of the priest to anoint the sick, and to pray for them, so that they may be restored to health. It is probably the least familiar of all the sacraments for many people, and it is still surrounded with a surprising amount of fear

> *...it remains one of the regular duties of the priest to anoint the sick, and to pray for them, so that they may be restored to health*

and superstition, so we need to explain precisely what it is, what it means, and how it works, so that those who are ill may ask for it with confidence, and those who care for the sick can understand what is happening, and what effects it is likely to have. We look also at the history of the sacrament, to show that contrary to popular opinion it has always been intended to be a moment of healing and consolation.

1. THE INCARNATE WORD: HEALING OF THE WHOLE PERSON

The fundamental affirmation of our faith is that the Word was made Flesh (*Jn* 1:14): this means that not only the human soul, but even the human body is caught up into the divine. The ancient philosophers thought that material things were unimportant, if not positively evil, and they imagined that only the mind, the reasoning soul, was capable of relating to the divine, that only the spiritual part of a human being was destined to survive death, the body was vile, and beneath God's notice. They were wrong in this, as in so much else: our God became flesh, a real human living breathing body, sprung from the earth which God had created, 'and He saw that it was good' (*Gen* 1:31). The human body is important, just as the rest of God's material creation is important, and the Incarnation of Jesus Christ means that we are united to God in body as well as soul. That is why we believe in the resurrection of the body: where Christ has gone before, we hope to follow, to be saved and redeemed, body and soul together. It is quite true that the body has its problems, it can rebel against our better nature, and St Francis called it 'Brother Ass', but Our Lord did ride into Jerusalem on Brother Ass.

As proof of this, when Our Lord preached in Galilee and Judea, His preaching was accompanied by the healing of physical illness. Not that He did this to impress people, still less to convince them of the truth of His Message. Whenever Our Lord cured someone, He gave them strict instructions to tell no one. Over and over again He appealed to them to keep quiet about the power of God in their lives - and occasionally they obeyed Him. (See *Matt* 9:30-31, *Mark* 1: 43-5, among other passages.) There were several reasons for this: one mentioned specifically by the Gospel writers is that Our Lord did not want to be mobbed by thousands of people crowding round in the hope of a cure, but with no interest in hearing the message. But more importantly, Our Lord tried to make people keep silent about His miracles because you cannot force people to believe by showing them signs and wonders. From time to time His opponents challenged Him to work a public miracle to prove His claim to authority, and He always refused, whether it was the devil who asked him (*Matt* 4:7) or the devout Pharisees (*Matt* 12:38-42). Those who believe already will certainly be reinforced and comforted in their faith by witnessing the marvels of God's grace, but

A leper came to him and pleaded on his knees: If you want to he said you can cure me . Feeling sorry for him, Jesus stretched out his hand and touched him. Of course I want to! he said. Be cured! And the leprosy left him at once and he was cured. (Mark 1:40-42)

those who do not believe will not believe even if someone should return from the dead (*Luke* 16:31).

Healing the wounds of sin and separation

Our Lord came to restore the breach between God and His Creation, to unite mankind to the divinity. Sickness, and suffering of all kinds, are ultimately the results of a rebellion against the order of God's creation, whether through our own sins, or through the disturbance of the balance of nature, leading to the separation and alienation of God and man. It is not often our own actual sins that cause our own suffering (though certainly it is sometimes), but the sins of other people, maybe people we have never met and know nothing about. A cancer may be caused by our own self-indulgence in smoking, or it may be the result of radiation left over from the atmospheric nuclear explosions of the 1950s. Some diseases can be traced directly to the maleficence of man, some remain inexplicable, but all are ultimately the result of the malice of the devil, magnified by the sins of ordinary people like you and me. When the disciples asked Our Lord whether it was the blind man himself or his parents who had sinned (*John* 9:2), Jesus refused to answer: we can hardly ever be explicit about whose sins it was that caused this particular instance of human suffering, but we can be confident that the solution is the glory of God. Our Lord's redemptive work must involve putting right what had been damaged by sin, which is why the healing of body, mind and spirit was so prominent a sign of His presence on earth.

Yet death remains the common lot of all mankind. Our Lord has conquered death, but we can only join his victory parade after we have passed the selfsame way. That is why no healing in this life is permanent: Lazarus rose, only to die again, and all those who are healed of one particular disease or injury will assuredly die one day. That is why for many the most valuable healing is the healing of mind, which enables them to pass through death in peace, a peace which is often shared with those around them. A great many of the healings performed by Our Lord were healings of the mind, of those who had been afflicted by the devil in some way. We might classify most of these cases as some form of mental illness, but are not really much closer to understanding our own curious behaviour at times than were Our Lord's contemporaries, who knew only that in some way the powers of evil had interfered in a person's mental well being, and knew that Our Lord could cure. The borderline between mental and physical illness is, after all, very narrow, and healing must involve the whole person. Once the mind is at rest, with the assurance of the love of God, then the body may recover, or the person move peacefully and quickly to a holy death, in order to rise again fully renewed in Christ. The Gospels speak of many people who were afflicted by the devil ('demonised'), but only very rarely of those who were actually 'possessed' or taken over by an alien intelligence, like the man at Gadara (*Mark* 5:1-20). These too, Our Lord could cure with a word, for He came to set us free from all evil.

Miracles as Signs

Although Our Lord refused to work miracles in order to impress people, He did refer to them as 'signs' to confirm the faith which his disciples already had. When John the Baptist in his prison began to become discouraged, He sent a message pointing to these signs, 'the blind see again, and the lame walk, lepers are cleansed, and the deaf hear, and the dead are raised to life, and the Good News is proclaimed to the poor.' (*Matt* 11:5) They are not signs that will convert the unwilling - when the chief priests hear of the raising of Lazarus their first instinct is to kill him all over again (*John* 12:11) - but for someone like John the Baptist, who does already believe, they are a welcome consolation and strengthening.

Jesus answered, Go back and tell John what you hear and see; the blind see again, and the lame walk, lepers are cleansed, and the deaf hear, and the dead are raised to life and the Good News is proclaimed to the poor; and happy is the man who does not lose faith in me . (Matt 11:4-6)

To perform miracles in public looks like doing tricks to impress people: Our Lord refused to do this, though everyone from the devil upwards begged him to do so. He cured people because He loved them: and He continues His healing work in the sacraments of the Church, simply because He loves us. The Apostles continued Our Lord's practice of trying to avoid publicity, as have all the saints ever since. In fact it is one of the ways you can tell a genuine saint from a fraud: the saints are always very shy about the works of healing done through them, try to conceal them as far as

> *Christ continues His healing work in the sacraments of the Church, simply because He loves us*

possible, and if that can't be done they try to attribute them to the prayers of someone else, as St John Vianney attributed all his miracles to St Philomena. The Sacrament of the Anointing of the Sick is, therefore, a hidden sacrament: one which many regularly practising Catholics may never have even witnessed.

2. A SACRAMENT FROM THE BEGINNING OF THE CHURCH

In several places in the Gospel, Our Lord tells us that he expects his disciples to do exactly the same things that He did, to cure the sick, cleanse lepers, raise the dead and preach to the poor (e.g. *Matt* 28:19, *Mark* 16:16-18, *Luke* 24:47, *John* 14:12). In the Acts of the Apostles we see them doing precisely that, continuing Our Lord's healing work, even as they continued to preach His message. In fact, they began this ministry even before the Crucifixion. In the Gospel of St Mark we read that Our Lord sent his disciples out to preach, and they anointed many sick people with oil, and cured them (*Mark* 6:7-13). We hear of the same practice in the Epistle of St James, where the Apostle recommends that the sick should call for the priests of the Church, who will anoint them and lay hands over them (*James* 5:14-15). The anointing with oil is therefore clearly attested in what many believe to be the two oldest

If one of you is ill, he should send for the elders of the church, and they must anoint him with oil in the name of the Lord and pray over him. The prayer of faith will save the sick man and the Lord will raise him up again; and if he has committed any sins, he will be forgiven. (James 5:14-15)

> The Sacrament is, therefore, made up of two natural human gestures, to signify the supernatural divine work of grace; anointing with oil and the laying on of hands.

documents of the New Testament. Why oil? We read of anointing with olive oil, sometimes scented, in many places in the Scriptures, usually as a sign of a special grace or a special vocation being conferred on someone (e.g. *I Sam* 16:13, *I Kings* 19:16). But there is nothing in the Old Testament specifically about anointing the sick. We need to remember that anointing the skin with olive oil was a familiar part of everyday life. Every time someone washed, they would afterwards rub oil onto the skin, as a protection against the sun and wind, and a healing for minor scratches and insect bites. The natural healing properties of olive oil, much exploited these days in natural remedies, meant that it was an obvious gesture to use when praying for the sick. It has certainly been so used from the time of the Apostles until now, even in societies and countries where olive oil is unfamiliar and exotic. The gesture of laying on hands is also a very natural sign of passing on energy, as we instinctively want to touch those who are suffering to reassure them of our concern. The Sacrament is, therefore, made up of two natural human gestures, to signify the supernatural divine work of grace.

The Church Fathers and the Sacrament of Anointing

Having said that, it must be admitted that we have little evidence on how the sacrament was used during the first eight centuries of the Church. References in the writings of the Church Fathers are few, and brief. Most place the anointing of the sick in the context of one of the means of finding forgiveness for sins, as the passage where Saint John Cassian collects Scriptural texts, including the passage from St James, chapter 5, to illustrate the 'many fruitful penances by which we may attain the forgiveness of sins' (*Collations,* XX, 8). We must remember that until late in the first millennium the actual sacrament of penance was a rare privilege, granted only to those who had seriously defected from the faith, and could normally only be granted once in a lifetime: for the remission of daily venial sins, regular confessions were made without formal absolution, not necessarily to a priest, and therefore for many the only opportunity for a priest to be instrumental in their forgiveness was in the anointing of the sick. Physical or mental healing were always seen as an aspect of the forgiveness of sins.

The most famous of early references to the sacrament, indeed the first to use the word 'sacrament' explicitly, is in a letter of AD 416 from Pope Innocent I to bishop Decentius of Gubbio. (*Mansi III,* 1,031; J. Neuner and J. Dupuis, *The Christian Faith* (1982), p

450). He speaks of the importance of the bishop who consecrates the oil, not only in order for a priest or bishop to use it for the anointing of the sick, but also so that lay people can use it. It was certainly the custom for lay people to possess quantities of the blessed oil, to anoint those who were sick, though it is also certain that this was seen as something different from the actual anointing of the sick done by a priest in accordance with the passage from St James. (The difference is nowadays made between a 'sacrament', such as baptism, and a 'sacramental' such as blessing ourselves or each other with holy water when entering a church or a Catholic home.) This is illustrated by the life of St Hypatius, a contemporary of Pope Innocent I, he was in the habit of picking up sick people he found lying around, and bringing them into his monastery to be tended: 'and if he saw that it were necessary that they be anointed with holy oil, he would tell the Abbot, who was a priest, and make sure that he anointed them; and it often happened that he could send them away cured a few days later.' (*Acta Sanctorum* June, Vol. IV, p. 251.) Pope Innocent goes on to say that those who have embarked on the sacrament of penance should not be anointed, because they cannot receive any of the other sacraments until they have been absolved. Hypatius and Pope Innocent are certainly not well-known Fathers of the Church, but they are valuable evidence for the practice of the early fifth century.

By the time of our own St Bede, in the early eighth century, regular confession with absolution had become a feature of church life, and so he is able to speak of the importance of giving the sick both sacraments. Shortly afterwards, Bishop Theodulf of Orleans, writing to his clergy in AD 798, tells them to make sure that the sick first receive the sacrament of penance, then that of anointing, and finally that of Holy Communion (*Capitular of Theodulf,* PL CV, 220). From then on the evidence is clear that the sacrament was a regular feature of church life, performed by a single priest, anointing the sick a number of times with olive oil blessed by a bishop. Significantly, however, in the Eastern Church, not yet separated from the West, it was customary for the priests themselves to bless the oil, and for the sacrament to be conferred by a number of priests together (remembering that St James says, 'send for the priests of the church' in the plural).

> *By the time of St Bede,… regular confession with absolution had become a feature of church life, and so he is able to speak of the importance of giving the sick both sacraments*

Scholastic Theology of the Sacraments

At the beginning of the second millennium, scholars began to write systematically about the sacraments, and for the first time really defined what a sacrament is, how many they are, how they should be performed, and what they achieve. The sacrament of anointing the sick was therefore defined at this period, clearly understood to be instituted by Christ (quoting Mark 6), and with the principal aim being the forgiveness of venial sins, the strengthening of mind and heart in face of the danger of death, and almost incidentally the mental and physical healing of the patient, if such were to be beneficial to the salvation of the soul. It was at this time that the sacrament came to be called *Extrema Unctio* or the 'Last Anointing', not only because it came last in the series of sacraments involving anointing which one might receive - baptism, confirmation, ordination - but also because it was the appropriate sacrament for those approaching death. We must remember that the Latin word *extrema* simply means the last in a series, and does not have any of the extreme connotations of the related English word.

Then he summoned the Twelve and began to send them out in pairs... So they set off to preach repentance; and they cast out many devils, and anointed many sick people with oil and cured them. (Mark 6:7, 12-13)

This phase of the development of Christian doctrine, the 'Scholastic' period, reaches its culmination in the writings of St Thomas Aquinas. He tells us that the Anointing is a true sacrament, instituted by Christ, and is properly conferred by anointing the five senses with the words 'through this holy anointing, may the divine mercy grant you the remission of sins.' Its effect is primarily to remove the spiritual weakness caused by past sins, secondarily to forgive any remaining actual sins; the physical healing is a side-effect, which happens if it would be beneficial towards the spiritual healing which is the main purpose of the sacrament. It can only be validly conferred by a priest (although anointing by a layperson may be a good devotional practice, a 'sacramental'), and can only be conferred on those who are seriously ill, and who are old enough to have been able to choose whether to sin or not. The senses are anointed because they have been the instruments of sin, and the sacrament may be repeated if the patient recovers and falls ill again, or even if there is a development in the progress of a single sickness. (*Supplementuum,* QQ xxix-xxxii).

Its effect is primarily to remove the spiritual weakness caused by past sins, secondarily to forgive any remaining actual sins; the physical healing is a side-effect, which happens if it would be beneficial towards the spiritual healing which is the main purpose of the sacrament.

Agreement and Disagreement

All of this was generally agreed, without controversy. In the various attempts to achieve reconciliation between the eastern and western Communions this was one of the many points on which full agreement was expressed, as at the Councils of Lyons and Florence, and the decrees of Pope Innocent III. Disagreement only came with the sixteenth-century revolt against church unity, when the various protestant bodies all agreed in rejecting the sacrament of anointing altogether. Luther contented himself by asserting it was a mere 'human invention', Calvin more roundly abused it as a 'histrionic hypocrisy', and the Anglican articles call it the 'corrupt following of the apostles.' In the face of such opposition the reforming Council of Trent had to look again at the Catholic understanding of the sacrament. The relevant decree, issued in 1551, speaks of it as 'the complement not only of penance but also of the whole Christian life', and a 'very strong safeguard' to protect the end of life. It repeats and confirms the teaching of St Thomas, and affirms the essential unity of contemporary practice with what is described in the New Testament. It is therefore wrong to despise it or hold it in contempt, and a grievous sin to defer it until the very last minute. (Session XIV, chapter 1, found for instance in J. Neuner and J. Dupuis, *The Christian Faith* (1982), pp. 465-71.)

The background to this controversy lies partly in the protestant rejection of the possibility of miracles - while not denying those recorded in the Gospels, they refused to believe that any miracle was possible after the end of the first century, and asserted that all miracles recorded in the history of the Church were frauds. If anointing the sick were to have the effect of curing them, this would contradict their position. St Thomas and the Council of Trent do not see miraculous cures as the main purpose of the sacrament, but they do recognise that such cures happen as a side-effect of the principal work of taking away the guilt and legacy of sin. The council was quite well enough aware of human nature to see that a physical cure can result from the comfort and strengthening received by assurance of God's mercy, 'strengthened by this, the sick person bears more lightly the inconveniences and trials of his illness.' Indeed, physical cures received as a result of the anointing of the sick were not usually regarded as miraculous, for Catholic theologians were not ignorant of the close links between soul, mind and body. The protestants had also revived the ancient philosophical system of Plato, with its sharp distinction between matter and spirit, and therefore denied any real value to the body, or any material thing. They could not see any value in physical healing, nor any connection between healing of mind and body, and therefore flatly denied that it ever happened.

Post-Tridentine Developments

There was little development in the following centuries, apart from pastoral rulings about the actual administration of the sacrament: although five or seven anointings were originally normal, it was established that at least two could regularly be omitted, and that in case of emergency one was quite sufficient. The prayers prescribed were to be shortened if necessary, though ideally the sacrament should still be administered with sufficient time available to perform it properly and without hurry. The 1917 code of Canon Law, summing up previous decisions, reminds priests that it should not be conferred on those who have clearly rejected God and the Church unless they show some sign of repentance, but those who have been accustomed to receive the sacraments should be anointed even if they are unconscious (*CIC* 942-3). Recognising implicitly the validity of the Eastern practice, it notes that the Holy See can grant permission for a priest to bless the oil himself (*CIC* 945).

At no stage in Christian history did the authority of the Church sanction the idea that the sacrament should be left until the last minute: Trent decrees it is to be administered 'to the sick, especially those who are so dangerously ill that they seem near to death', but clearly not excluding an earlier phase of illness. The fact that St Thomas envisages the sacrament being repeated whenever the illness takes another turn shows that he understood that it can be given at the beginning of a long and complicated illness. Nevertheless, the state of medical attention available to most people before the twentieth century meant that the first onset of any serious illness was usually the prelude to an early death. It was popular superstition and ignorance, akin to the general reluctance to call in a doctor until all hope was lost, that made people defer the sacrament to the last minute, and has left an unchanged legacy of suspicion against what romantic novelists have dubbed the 'last rites'. Nothing any Church authority has said, whether in the middle ages or since, has put a stop to this ignorance, and still most people try to avoid letting a priest know about an illness in the family until it is too late. In this respect, the second Vatican council has had no effect whatever.

> *Vatican II did not envisage any substantial change in the understanding of the sacrament, other than to recommend the name 'anointing of the sick' as an alternative to 'extreme unction'*

Recent Times

Vatican II did not envisage any substantial change in the understanding of the sacrament, other than to recommend the name 'anointing of the sick' as an alternative to 'extreme unction'. It repeats what the Council of Trent said about it being appropriate at the beginning of a life-threatening illness, not only towards the end, and retains the order of sacraments described by Theodulf, confession, anointing and Holy Communion. It also ratified the existing practice of varying the number of anointings depending on the condition of the sick person, with appropriate prayers (*Sacrosanctum Concilium* 73-5). Early twentieth-century thinking about the sacrament was formed by the authoritative work of Joseph Kern, and the fathers of Vatican II clearly followed that thinking.

The subsequent new rite of anointing, published in 1972, does mark a very clear break with the past, in that the removal of the consequences of sin no longer appears to be considered the principal effect. In the crucial form of words, forgiveness of sin is mentioned only in passing, in the past tense; translated literally it says, 'may [the Lord] save you who have already been delivered from your sins, and may he mercifully relieve you'. The principal effect is therefore help and relief, not forgiveness of sin, which it is to be assumed has already happened through the sacrament of penance. Another radical break with the past was the abolition of the anointing of the five senses, in favour of a simple anointing of forehead and hands. The new rite also introduces the unprecedented possibility of oil of another type being used, and also evisages that the priest can bless the oil without special authority if there is a real necessity to do so. In common with many of the new rites, it is presented in a form suitable only for communal liturgical celebration, with readings and a responsorial psalm, and therefore has to be adapted for individual use, even though in practice nearly always such an adaptation is necessary.

3. The Rite of Anointing the Sick

For many Catholics, the anointing of the sick is the one sacrament which they have never witnessed, for it usually takes place only in the privacy of a home or a hospital. It is therefore worth describing it in detail, and demonstrating how it should be understood.

The Old Rite of Extreme Unction

Firstly, let us look at the old rite, as it was used for most of the history of the Church. It is assumed that the sick person will be in a private room, which is unfortunately far from the case. Ideally there should be a table with a white cloth, a crucifix, and a candle. The priest arrives carrying the oil in a 'stock', which is usually a small round metal container with a tight-fitting screw top, containing a pad of cotton-wool soaked in the oil. He places the stock on the table, greets all present and sprinkles holy water. He may then hear the patient's sacramental confession, if this has not already been done. There follow three prayers asking for God's blessing on the place and all present, asking specifically for peace of mind: 'May he leave them no cause for fear or uneasiness of mind; and may he have them all in his safe keeping.' There follows the usual penitential rite from the Mass, after which the priest lays his right hand on the head of the sick person and prays for deliverance from all evil. The anointing then follows: opening the stock, the priest dips the ball of his right thumb in the oil, and anoints the sick person with the sign of the cross, on the eyelids, ears, nostrils, mouth and hands, each time saying, 'Through this holy anointing, and his most tender mercy, may the Lord forgive you whatever sins you have committed through your sense of [sight, etc].' The rubrics require him to wipe the oil away afterwards, each time with a fresh pad of cotton wool, which is afterwards to be taken back to church for reverent disposal. After the anointing follows the Lord's Prayer, and three more prayers, quoting the key text from St James, and including the astonishingly confident prayer for healing: 'Bind up his wounds; forgive his sins; rid him of all anguish of mind and body. Restore in thy mercy full health to his body and soul, so that with thy help he may be well again and able to take up his work again and his duties in life... let him feel now that thy healing hand has taken his suffering away... Give him health anew. Stretch out thy hand and set him on his feet again. Put strength into him, and keep him safe under thy powerful protection. Give him back to thy holy Church; and may all henceforth be well with him.' (Needless to say, if a woman is being anointed, all the prayers must be put into the feminine gender, demanding some skill with Latin when the sacrament was normally administered in that sacred language!)

Now, from all that, it is quite obvious that the old rite of anointing, Extreme Unction, was certainly not intended to be the last rite for those on the point of death. The forgiveness of sins is indeed the principal effect expected, and since sacramental confession has already been made and absolution given, it is obvious that it is not so much the guilt of the sins but the lingering effects that are being taken away, as well as the ceaseless daily dust of venial imperfections. Unlike the sacrament of penance, the formula is not a statement, 'I absolve you', but a prayer, 'may the Lord forgive you'. This does not imply any doubt in the Lord's intention to forgive, but it does allow latitude in the state of disposition of the patient. After all, the patient may very well not be totally conscious during all this, and may indeed be absolutely unconscious. It has to be assumed that the patient would ask for the sacrament if fully conscious, but there may well be some lingering attachment to sins which would present some obstacle to the Lord's mercy. The prayer is therefore to some extent conditional. The following prayers, with their confident demand for immediate physical and mental healing, do not sound at all conditional, but of course, like every prayer we ever make, they must include the silent condition, 'as thy will is, not as mine is' (*Matt* 26:39). As we have already mentioned, the understanding of the Church was always that a physical healing was to be expected only if it would be beneficial to the eternal salvation of the soul.

I have included all this about the old rite in an attempt to dispel the popular illusion that it used to be simply a last-minute sacrament after which there could be no hope of recovery for the sick person. That superstition was an abuse then as now, and responsible pastoral writers made exactly the same points that we do nowadays: the sacrament should be given when the sickness first becomes alarming, and may be repeated if there is a significant change. Indeed it was recommended that in the course of a long illness it could be repeated once a month. Moreover it was recommended for old people who were simply frail with no specific illness. (See the article in the 1907 *Catholic Encyclopedia*.)

The New Rite

To turn to the rite of 1972, which has been the most familiar in our time. Provision is made for it to take place in a hospital or private room, though ideally it is envisaged as taking place in church, preferably in the context of Mass. As such it is, of course, a familiar part of the proceedings at Lourdes, and some parishes do make a practice of having a Mass for the sick with anointing, for instance during the local diocesan pilgrimage to Lourdes. This means that any Catholic ought to have an opportunity of witnessing the sacrament, though, as I have said, in practice many have never seen it done until they come to stand round the bed of a seriously ill relation.

Public Celebration of the Rite

In the case of such a public celebration, almost by definition those present are not very seriously ill, and indeed there is a danger that it becomes rather trivialised by anointing everyone present on the grounds that there is nearly always something wrong with all of us. The General Instruction is still quite clear that it is intended for those seriously ill, or the frail and old, though without needing to be too scrupulous about whether there is a real danger of death or not. The Mass can be that of the day, particularly if it is a Sunday, or readings can be chosen from those provided in the lectionary for the sick. After the gospel and sermon, there is a litany of intercessions, to which all reply, and then the priest or priests lay hands on the heads of the sick, and anoint them on the forehead and hands. The Mass then proceeds with the general intercessions ('bidding prayers'), and concludes with an appropriate form of final blessing. If there are large numbers of people needing to be anointed, as can often happen during a pilgrimage, several priests may be needed to ensure that everyone is anointed within a reasonable time (remembering that the sick tire easily). Conversely, if there are only a few patients and more than one priest, all the priests present may lay on hands, though only one says the words and performs the anointing. What is not possible under any circumstances is for any one other than a priest or bishop to confer the sacrament.

Private Celebration

Far more common in our experience is the use of this sacrament for a single sick person, in their own bedroom or a hospital ward. This means that the rite has to be drastically adapted, taking into account not only the patient but also the family and friends, as well as hospital staff and other patients present. If you know of a Catholic patient in hospital, who is seriously ill, or about to undergo an operation, you have to find a way of delicately suggesting that they might like to receive the sacrament of the sick. It needs to be delicate, because the old superstition about 'last rites' has not died. Some such phrase as 'would you like me to give you the blessing of the sick?' or even 'a special blessing', may be necessary, adding immediately that it is a 'Very powerful prayer for healing. The oil we use was blessed specially by the bishop and all the priests of the diocese, so they are all praying together for you.' It is unfortunately rare to find a Catholic patient sufficiently well informed to ask directly for the 'Sacrament of Anointing'. They usually have to be gently brought up to the point that you can explain what is going on.

Not everyone in hospital need be anointed: many are in for very routine treatments, which are in no way life-threatening, and could not possibly be called serious. On the other hand, if anyone is very worried and anxious even about a routine treatment, the sacrament would be appropriate, to relieve the anxiety and reassure them of God's love. In some cases, for instance in an Ear Nose & Throat ward, people may be undergoing a simple routine operation which prevents them from swallowing for a few days, so if they would otherwise have been receiving Holy Communion, the Sacrament of the Sick might be appropriate as an alternative. The basic need is for sensitivity to the particular person and the particular occasion.

All this is from the point of view of the relations or the chaplain: if you are a patient in hospital, have no hesitation in asking directly to be anointed, because after reading this pamphlet you will be adequately informed as to what it is for!

The ideal moment for the sacrament is before an operation, not afterwards. It is routine that patients preparing for anaesthetic must not receive anything by mouth (the famous 'Nil by Mouth' notice over the bed), so they should not receive Holy Communion, but can and should be anointed. However in the present state of British hospitals, chaplains are no longer routinely informed about the admission of a Catholic patient, so they cannot usually find them in time to anoint them before the operation. It really is up to the patient, or their family, to notify the chaplain (best done through your own parish priest) as some hospital trusts are very hostile to the presence of Catholic priests, and cannot be relied on to pass on messages. It is, of course, far better to ask the priest to call in while the patient is still at home, when a decent and respectful atmosphere can more easily be maintained.

In a Hospital Ward

When it is necessary to confer the sacrament in a public hospital, it will probably not be possible to ensure privacy. Curtains can be drawn around the bed, and any family members present invited to cluster round. It is not possible to light candles, because of the presence of oxygen and smoke detectors, and it is rare to be able to clear a space for a white cloth and a crucifix. Often the crucifix and the oil stock simply have to be placed on the bedclothes. The priest should wear a purple stole, usually the miniature 'administration' stole, over his cassock or suit, and get as close as he can to the patient. If the patient is unconscious, it is still important for him to give a few words of explanation to the family and friends if they are there. It is not usually possible to rely on them to answer responses, still less to plan and choose readings as the rite imagines: however well-informed people may be, they are usually unnerved in the presence of serious illness, and in no state of mind to talk about choosing liturgical texts. If they are at all in touch with the Church they will at least make the sign of the cross to begin with, which is a useful indicator to the priest on how far he can expect them to join in. Usually they stand around in embarrassed silence. But it is good that they should be present, as the sacrament does have an effect on the bystanders as well.

The rite provides for a greeting and sprinkling with holy water, followed by an exhortation, quoting the text from the letter of St James, then the penitential rite as at Mass (the 'I confess...') and another scriptural reading. Often much of this has to be omitted, and we begin almost straightaway with the 'litany'. This is printed in the form of a succession of invocations, to which all present are supposed to make a regular response. Realistically, the invocations can be run together to make a continuous prayer, during which the priest lays his hand of the head of the patient:

> Lord, through this holy anointing, come and comfort [name] with your love and mercy; free her from all harm; relieve the sufferings of all the sick here present; assist all those dedicated to the care of the sick; free [name] from sin and all temptation; give life and health to our sister on whom we lay our hands in your name.

The head may not always be accessible, through various items of medical equipment, but the priest gets his hand as close as possible. The laying on of hands is not meant to be a dramatic gesture, but simply a consoling touch. In fact throughout the rite it may be useful for a family member or the priest to hold the patient's hand to maintain contact.

There follows a prayer over the oil, which also is supposed to have a response, but usually has to be said continuously:

> Praise to you, almighty God and Father; you sent your Son to live among us and bring us salvation; praise to you, Lord Jesus Christ, the Father s only Son, you humbled yourself to share in our humanity, and you desired to cure all our illnesses; praise to you, God the Holy Spirit, the Consoler, you heal our sickness with your mighty power. Blessed be God! Lord God, with faith in you, our sister will be anointed with this holy oil: ease her sufferings and strengthen her in her weakness. We ask this through Christ our Lord.

The priest then dips his thumb into the oil stock, and makes the sign of the cross with the oil on the forehead of the patient (or as near as he can get), saying:

> Through this holy anointing, may the Lord in his love and mercy help you with the grace of the Holy Spirit. Amen.

He then anoints the hands, if possible, saying:

> May the Lord who frees you from sin save you and raise you up. Amen.

The new rite does not specify whether it is to be the palms of the hands or the back that is anointed: the backs are usually much more accessible. (In the old rite it was explicitly the palms for a lay person, the backs for a priest.) Nor does the new rite say the oil should be wiped off again, and there seems to be little point in so doing.

There follows a prayer, one of a selection of which the first is this:

> Lord Jesus Christ, our Redeemer, by the power of the Holy Spirit, ease the suffering of our sick sister, and make her well again in mind and body. In your loving kindness forgive her sins, and grant her full health, so that she may be restored to your service. You are Lord for ever and ever.

After this comes the Lord's Prayer, which is usually the one thing the family and friends can easily join in. Often it seems natural to go on and say the Hail Mary as well, for it is good for them to join in as much as possible, and at this stage the reassuring and healing strength of the sacrament has usually become obvious.

If the condition of the patient allows (and it usually doesn't) this is the moment to give Holy Communion, after which there is a final blessing for the patient and all present.

In Emergency

Conditions may be even less ideal than that; when the patient is quite unconscious, in an intensive care unit, or even on a theatre trolley, the priest may have no one to accompany him (except, quite often, a Catholic nurse), and has to abbreviate even more, reducing it to the prayer accompanying the laying on of hands, the actual anointing prayer (which is essential) and the one immediately afterwards, with the Our Father: and it is worth whispering that into the patient's ear, because often people hear more than you could imagine. When the family and friends have refused to be present and witness the sacrament, it is still important that the priest should have a brief word with them, to reassure them that he has given what the Church offers for the healing and well-being of the patient. If they are not present it is routine to ask the staff to make a note that the priest has been, since family are often anxious about that, even if they have no apparent faith themselves. For many, the appearance of the priest at the bedside is their first contact with the Catholic Church, if the patient herself has been out of touch with the Church, and the next generation were never in touch. A lot can depend on the impression made during those few moments.

Theology of the Sacrament

Looking at the old and new prayers for blessing the oil also gives us an insight into the two theologies of the sacrament. The original blessing was always done on Maundy Thursday, by the bishop in his cathedral, at a special Mass which was not normally attended by a congregation. The blessing came at the end of the canon, just before the Our Father, which was the original position in the Mass for all sorts of blessings of things offered to God. The text is explicit that the oil is set aside and dedicated to God's service, and that a particular power of healing is infused into it. The oil is brought to the bishop by one of the subdeacons, and the bishop blesses it with two prayers, first cleansing the oil:

> so that it can become a spiritual anointing to strengthen the temple of the living God (i.e. the human body),

And then proceeding to call down the Holy Spirit onto the oil:

> which you have been pleased to produce for us from the evergreen tree, for the refreshment of mind and body, so that through your holy benediction it may become a safeguard of mind and body for everyone who is anointed with this oil of heavenly medicine, in order to expel all pain and weakness, and every disease of mind or body, just as you anointed priests, kings, prophets and martyrs, may it be, O Lord, a perfect ointment blessed for us by you, and remaining in our midst.

It is noticeable that in this blessing there is no mention of the forgiveness of sins, but the oil is explicitly and confidently blessed as a 'heavenly medicine' for healing. (The other two oils, of Catechumens and of Chrism, are blessed after the Communion of the Mass, with very much more dramatic ceremonial.)

Changes in the new Rite

In the new rite, the blessing is not invoked on the oil itself, so much as on the people who will be anointed with it, in line with the theology of the 1970s which avoids speaking of the possibility of sanctifying material objects. Along with the other two oils, it is done after the Gospel at the Chrism Mass, which is celebrated by the bishop or his deputy some time shortly before Easter, and is attended by a representative congregation from every parish of the diocese. The new text reads:

> Lord God, loving Father, you bring healing to the sick through your Son, Jesus Christ. Hear us as we pray to you in faith, and send the Holy Spirit, man s helper and friend, upon this oil, which nature has provided to serve the needs of men. May your blessing come upon all who are anointed with this oil, that they may be freed from pain and illness and made well again in body, mind, and soul. Father, may this oil be blessed for our use in the name of our Lord Jesus Christ who lives and reigns with you for ever and ever.

Here again there is no mention of the forgiveness of sins, and the purpose of the anointing is seen purely as that of healing. The prayer has been simplified and shorn of its picturesque language, but essentially it does say the same as the prayer in the old rite.

As in all the sacraments, the Holy Trinity is invoked, calling on the Father in the name of Jesus His Son, in the power of the Holy Spirit. It is the Spirit who is called down upon the oil, just as the gesture of laying on of hands is always seen as an invocation of the Holy Spirit. The effect of the sacrament is the work of God, not the priest, nor those around, nor the patient. Nor is there any natural healing power in the oil itself: although olive oil does indeed have mild healing properties, the quantity used could not possibly have a natural therapeutic effect. The oil is used as a symbol, chosen because of its value as a soothing and healing medium, but as in every sacrament, the symbol is the outward sign of an invisible action on the part of God.

The sacraments are the fruit of faith, but it is the faith of the entire Church, not of any individual. This means that it does not matter at all whether the patient believes in the power of the sacrament, as long as she is open to receiving some grace

> *The effect of the sacrament is the work of God, not the priest, nor those around, nor the patient*

from God through the Church; it does not matter whether the priest is aware of the meaning of the sacrament, or believes it will have any effect, as long as he intends to do what the Church does. The patient may be totally unconscious, and the priest drunk and irreverent, but the sacrament depends on the faith of the Church and is God's guaranteed response to the action of the Church. Obviously it is highly desirable that both priest and patient should be devout and in a state of grace, but they should not imagine that they have to work themselves up into a mental condition when they really really believe they are going to be cured in order for it to take effect. God's grace is not dependent on human effort, luckily. When people are cured after receiving the sacrament of anointing it is nothing to do with the holiness of either priest or patient, nor with their mental state at the time: it is God's free grace.

Form and Matter

In this sacrament, therefore, the 'form', the prescribed prayer which the Church asks her priest to use, is the key text:

> Through this holy anointing, may the Lord in his love and mercy help you with the grace of the Holy Spirit. May the Lord who frees you from sin save you and raise you up. Amen.

Although this form is new, and quite different from that accepted by all previous theologians and Church authorities, it comes to us on the apostolic authority of Pope Paul VI. The same apostolic authority could change it in the future, either back to the old form or to a new one, but at present that form, duly promulgated by authority, is

Scholastic theologians analysed sacraments in terms of matter and form. The matter is the visible element or symbolic gesture, such as anointing with oil. The form is the actual words or prayer used, which brings out the significance of and makes explicit what is already there.

the one the Church requires us to use. If we try to make up one for ourselves it might be a very beautiful prayer, but it would not be a sacrament of the Church.

The 'matter' of the sacrament, likewise, is the anointing with oil. The oil itself is the 'remote matter', existing in itself independently of the priest. From the very beginning it has been olive oil, which, as I have mentioned, has associations with healing, cleansing, preserving, and lighting, as well as cooking. The natural symbolism of the oil can draw on all these (well, maybe not cooking), and the associations that we find in the Scriptures. The use of oil as a sign of power and authority in the Old Testament derives from these associations, as well as from the value of the oil, and the influence which comes from possessing a supply of oil. We should be very careful, therefore, about taking advantage of the concession in the 1972 rite to use other forms of vegetable oil: cheap salad or frying oil has no association other than culinary, and the rare and expensive 'essential oils' used for alternative medicine have only the one association, and that one is often tied in with alternative theological and mystical ideas which are out of place in the Catholic Church. The quantity of oil needed for anointing the sick does not impose an unreasonable financial burden on any diocese in the modern world, costing no more than wine which has always been considered absolutely essential for the Mass.

The 'proximate matter' of the sacrament is the actual anointing. For this it is important that the oil actually touches the skin of the person, and that it is administered by the priest himself without using any instrument or barrier. A sacrament is a personal contact with Our Lord, in the person of His priest, and nothing should come between Christ and the people He loves. Having said that, necessary health precautions should be taken: the priest should be prepared to gown up if required, and to wash his hands with antiseptic gel before and after contact with the patient, if the medical authorities advise it. No precise quantity of oil is prescribed, but the amount that will naturally be carried on the ball of the thumb after it has been dipped in the oil stock is sufficient to trace a cross about five centimetres wide on the skin of the patient. The priest may find after a few years that his administration stole and the pages of his book are thoroughly impregnated with the oil, but in itself it is not consecrated in the way that the Blessed Sacrament is, and it is not necessary to take extraordinary precautions over its disposal. On the other hand it should not be treated with disrespect: if the oil is

> *A sacrament is a personal contact with Our Lord, in the person of His priest, and nothing should come between Christ and the people He loves*

wiped off with cotton wool, it is better to dispose of it reverently (buried or burned) rather than simply chucking it into the sluice. At the end of the year the oil stocks are cleaned out, and the remaining oil and cotton wool burned, before stocking up with the newly blessed oil at Easter.

4. Visible Effects of the Sacrament

A sacrament, by definition, is an outward and visible sign of an inward and spiritual grace: we should not normally expect, therefore, to see any external visible sign that a sacrament has taken effect. A baptised baby looks and behaves in exactly the same way as before; consecrated bread and wine suffer absolutely no external change which can be detected by the most searching examination. Nevertheless, in the one case of the sacrament of Anointing the Sick, external visible effects are so common, that they can almost be invoked as evidence and witness to the invisible effects of the other sacraments.

Our Lord Himself did on occasion point to the visible effect of a physical cure, as evidence for the invisible, but much more important, effect of the forgiveness of sins. When they brought him a paralysed man on a stretcher, Jesus said first of all, 'your sins are forgiven'. He waited while the bystanders took this in, and began, predictably, to express their surprise and disapproval - 'who can forgive sins but God?' - and then proceeded to rebuke their lack of faith. Which is easier to say, 'your sins are forgiven', or, 'rise up and walk'? Anyone could claim to forgive sins in the name of God, and no one would be any the wiser, but it is a courageous and confident man who then goes on to say to the paralysed man, 'rise and walk', which of course Our Lord did, to prove 'that the Son of Man has authority on earth to forgive sins'. (*Matt* 9:5-8, and parallels) Our Lord worked many miracles of healing, both of mind and body, and he also forgave the sins of those who came to him in repentance. Our own practice is something of the reverse: we priests are continually employed in the confessional, pronouncing absolution for sins, giving people the invisible intangible assurance of God's love; less often are we called on to confer the sacrament of anointing, which so often has the visible effect of healing in mind or body.

Remarkable Effects

Every priest who is experienced in the use of this sacrament could tell amazing stories about its effect, but no sensible priest would do so. To describe individual cases, specifying names, places and dates, would be an unwarranted intrusion into the privacy of the patient and all concerned. That is why you should not expect to find

> Now, which of these is easier: to say, Your sins are forgiven , or to say Get up and walk But to prove to you that the Son of Man has authority on earth to forgive sins, - he said to the paralytic - get up, and pick up your bed and go off home . And the man got up and went home. A feeling of awe came over the crowd when they saw this, and they praised God for giving such power to men (Matt 9:5-8)

detailed accounts of cures resulting from the use of this sacrament. But that is not to say they do not happen.

Admittedly, in older lives of the saints, or Christian biographies, we do not often read much about the sacrament. This is because the authors are usually concerned to emphasise the holiness of the person they are describing, and want us to attribute the healing to their personal intercession with God, rather than the intercession of the entire Church mediated through the sacrament. Thus in Antonio Gallonio's Life of St Philip Neri, for instance, we read of many cases of the sick being so near to death that they had actually received the Sacrament of Extreme Unction, but at the last minute they were cured after Philip had laid hands on them. The priest who had administered the sacrament is not usually noticed. In the most famous story, that of the raising of Paolo Massimo, we read that the local priest, Don Camillo, had been to see the dying boy, had heard his confession and anointed him, but that what was really essential was a visit from Philip Neri, who raised him from death in order to speak to him for a while and to commend him to a peaceful death. (A. Gallonio, *Vita Sancti Philippi Neri,* para. 125, in *Acta Sanctorum* May, Vol. VI, 493.) There is no suggestion that the sacrament of anointing had any part either in the miraculous revival, or in the forgiveness of sins. It appears therefore, that at least in the mind of Antonio Gallonio, the sacrament was no more than a final commendation of a dying soul, despite the clear evidence of the texts used in blessing the oil and in conferring the sacrament and the teaching of the recent Council of Trent.

Very different is the approach of Father Martindale, who writes, 'Probably every priest who has often given this sacrament to the dying, has noticed the amazing change that it operates both in the bodily well-being of the sick person, and, above all, in the peace of mind which is one of its fruits. We have ourselves been asked, by non-Catholic nurses in a hospital, whether we could not give it also to non-Catholics, such were its visibly good effects. It is related that once, during the war, a priest crawled out into No Man's Land, to anoint wounded men who could not be brought in. So profound a silence and calm followed the groaning that had been heard before, that a non-Catholic officer thought that the priest had administered a narcotic drug, and asked for some for himself.' (C.C. Martindale, *The Last Sacraments & Prayers for the Dying,* CTS 1946, p. 3.)

A modern hospital chaplain, and for that matter presumably a military chaplain, has certainly experienced the same remarkable effects of the sacrament. It is safe to say that there is always some effect, but it is absolutely unpredictable. The sacraments are not magic, and we cannot force God to do things for us. What he does is guarantee a gift of grace in response to the faith of the

Church expressed in the sacrament. In the old rite, we remember, this grace, which is always given, was clearly defined as the grace of forgiveness of unconfessed venial sins, and the removal of the lingering traces of sin: the grace of healing was conditional in relation to the principal aims of the sacrament. The new rite, saying so much less about forgiveness, expects a healing grace as the invariable consequence of the sacrament. Few are disappointed, though the nature of the healing is, as I said, totally unpredictable.

> *...a healing grace [is expected] as the invariable consequence of the sacrament. Few are disappointed, though the nature of the healing is, as I said, totally unpredictable*

Healing the whole Person

Healing takes place on every level of the complex human person, in soul, mind and body. Each has its effect on the other, so that it is usually impossible to say to what extent the sacrament has affected the patient, for some aspects of the healing process are purely natural, while others can certainly be called supernatural. The healing of soul is still primarily a matter of repairing the damage caused by sin. Even sins that have been confessed and absolved can leave a legacy of guilt and anxiety, and it was always considered a specific purpose of the sacrament to remove this legacy. This removal of guilt and anxiety in turn relieves the mind, and helps people to relax and be at peace. When we anoint people who are conscious, they most often comment afterwards, 'I feel so much better now'; we can usually observe that they are more at ease, and more confident. This is perhaps especially noticeable when they have been anointed before undergoing an operation: the natural anxiety and dread in face of the anaesthetic and the scalpel so often seems to diminish or disappear, and they look positively cheerful after receiving the sacrament.

This effect is also very noticeable among the relatives and bystanders. Very often in fact they are much more worried than the patient, and it can be a major concern to make sure that they do not pass their anxieties on to the one actually undergoing the operation. Giving them peace of mind and confidence in the love of God is an important aspect of the healing work of the Church.

Now of course we can say that this effect may be purely natural. It is characteristic of the way in which a priest operates that we do not go in for dramatic gestures and impressive declamations: there are no chantings, dancings, waving around of strange objects, such as we hear of in many non-Catholic 'healing' ceremonies. It is all done in a straightforward and matter-of-fact way: the priest arrives, has a few words of compassion to say to the patient and the relatives, may explain very briefly what is going on, and then administers the sacrament very quietly and gently. The laying on of hands and the anointing are no more than a gentle touch, as one might caress a dear friend. It is precisely because the sacrament is administered in this calm and assured way that it produces the effect of assurance and calm. In this aspect, the priest's bedside manner has to be like that of a doctor: if the doctor rushes in, tears his hair and shouts out, 'Oh how terrible!' before going on to make a great song and dance about the treatment he is offering, he is not going to inspire much confidence: we feel much more at ease when the doctor speaks calmly and gently.

Being put at ease, acquiring calm and peace of mind, is of course the best way of ensuring that any physical treatment will be successful. We hear so much these days about stress: everyone knows that if you relieve stress and remove anxiety, the physical symptoms can be so much more easily cured. In many cases, indeed, the physical symptoms have no other cause than stress: there is little point in medicines or surgery if the underlying stress remains, because the symptoms will simply reappear all over again. That observation is not a modern insight, as I have already noticed: the Council of Trent was well aware that the physical healing which so often follows the anointing of the sick may be the result of the comfort and strengthening received through assurance of God's mercy. That is why we cannot usually say that the physical recovery of those who have been anointed is miraculous. They receive the sacrament, and they go into the operating theatre relaxed and confident, all goes well, and they are discharged from hospital in due course.

Those who do not recover

And of course, there are those who do not recover, for no one would wish to live for ever, and the time comes for all to be set free from the troubles of this world. For some people, it is actually anxiety and fear that makes them unable to die: the natural effect of being reassured and comforted with the assurance of God's love means that they can relax and fall asleep in Our Father's arms. Again this effect of peace and freedom from anxiety is so often transmitted to the relatives. They are able to accept the death of the one they love, and often comment on how peaceful and happy they looked at the last. This is particularly important when the patient is already unconscious. It often happens that we are called into the intensive care unit to see someone who is probably already dead. The body is kept going by a marvellous array of machines, and no one can really be sure when death occurs. It is traditional to perform a number of tests, and only after the patient fails to respond to the last test are the machines actually disconnected. This process can be particularly beneficial to the family, especially in the case of a sudden accident or haemorrhage, for it gives them time to collect their thoughts, and to come to terms with what is happening. Here administering the sacrament of anointing often seems to make a great difference to the family. They can pass from terrified denial to a calm acceptance, and can say their farewells to the one they love, comforted by the knowledge that God loves them as well.

Of course everyone has the freedom to accept or reject the grace of God, and there are always some who do not want to know about God's love. They may experience nothing of this healing, and may look on the priest's visit as no more than an irrelevant intrusion on the family's private resentment. If the patient is conscious and refuses to receive the sacrament, there is nothing we can do. If the patient is unconscious, and the family refuse to let the priest visit, again there is nothing we can do. It does often happen that a family keeps the priest away until after the patient is dead, and then sends for him. They will have to take responsibility for the fact that they may have deprived their loved one of the chance of recovery, certainly deprived her of any comfort at the end. Once someone is dead, no sacrament can be given. We can and do pray for the repose of their soul, but the relatives cannot be fobbed off by performing meaningless rituals over a corpse, if they have refused us access while the patient is still alive.

But when the family does have faith, even the proverbial grain of mustardseed's worth, then we can and do pray with them after the patient has died, perhaps saying the prayers to commend a departed soul or getting them to join in a decade of the rosary. That is not part of the sacramental life of the Church, but regular pastoral care. That is why if a patient dies after having received all the sacraments, happy and peaceful in the odour of sanctity, the priest is still normally called out to pray with the family afterwards. When the hospital calls to say that someone is already dead, we tend to go when the family are there, not before. We can pray for the repose of a soul anywhere: visiting the bedside is only necessary when there are survivors to console.

Physical Healing

But not all die, and not all healings are purely natural. It happens so often that we are not surprised, so rarely that we are still stricken with awe, that a patient after anointing makes a sudden and inexplicable recovery. The moment when the oil touches the forehead can be marked by a reaction ranging from a gentle opening of the eyes, to leaping out of bed with a roar. I must admit that sometimes I can't resist watching the monitor screen at the moment of anointing, to see if there is a sudden change in the lines traced across it. That does not seem to happen, but it certainly does happen that the unconscious patient in intensive care may be found the next morning sitting up in an ordinary ward having tea. They are usually rather embarrassed and sheepish about it, the priest even more so. Some have been out of touch with the Church for some time: when you ask them if they would like Holy Communion they (rightly) say that they haven't been to confession for a long time, and ought to do that first. And they don't really take it in when you tell them they were actually absolved of their sins last night, and the proof of that is that they are now sitting up and will soon be leaving hospital. 'To prove to you that the Son of Man on earth has power to forgive sins, rise, take up your bed and walk.'

> *We know that the sacrament has some effect every time, but whether that effect will be to prepare them for a quick and peaceful death, or to send them out to a prolonged and useful life we cannot tell until afterwards*

Why do some recover, and some not? To that question there is no answer. God's ways are not our ways. We can see no reason why a very elderly lady who has been a regularly practising Catholic should make a recovery and go on for years, to the considerable inconvenience and expense of those who have to care for her, while a young mother with an eighteen-month child does not recover. Sometimes we can observe that it is the 'lapsed', the out-of-touch, who recover, given more time to reform their lives; but as often it is the good who as far as we can see have no further need of earthly penance. It is inexplicable, and unpredictable. We know that the sacrament has some effect every time, but whether that effect will be to prepare them for a quick and peaceful death, or to send them out to a prolonged and useful life we cannot tell until afterwards.

And, you know, many of those who are cured after receiving the sacrament are not in the least bit grateful. We remember the ten lepers whom Our Lord cured, and there was only one who bothered to come back and give thanks. Once the initial shock has worn off, they will tell their friends, 'Of course, the priest came and did his thing, but despite that I recovered.' They go off happily believing that that recovery was entirely due to their own cleverness and strength of will, and had nothing at all to do with the priest's visit. And of course it has nothing at all to do with the priest: he is simply the channel through which God operates, and he can claim no more credit for the work of the sacrament than a hospital orderly who administers some powerful new drug can claim credit for its medicinal effects. A sacrament is the work of God, given and guaranteed in response to the prayer of the entire Church: the minister of the sacrament has no personal function at all.

FURTHER READING

There really is not much to recommend on this sacrament, which remains largely unknown to many Catholics. A search through the catalogue of one of our major libraries fails to find anything specifically published on this sacrament since Vatican II. It is treated, of course, in all general works on the Faith, and on the Sacraments, but usually very briefly. The great *Catechism of the Catholic Church*, for instance, gives it seven pages (paras. 1499 to 1525). For a detailed theological study we have to return to the massive work by Joseph Kern, *De Sacramento Extremae Unctionis Tractatus Dogmaticus* (Ratisbon 1907), which is summarised in English by P. J. Toner in the old *Catholic Encyclopedia* (V, 716-30). Another learned German, B. Poschmann, was published in English as *Penance and the Anointing of the Sick* in 1964. A short tract by J. P. Arendzon, *Extreme Unction,* appeared as part of the 'Treasury of the Faith' series and was reprinted in *The Teaching of the Catholic Church* edited by George Smith, 1948. Other works, in languages other than English, deal with it purely from a historical, or canonical standpoint.

On the Sacraments:

Baptism (CTS Publications, 2004; Do 712).
Confirmation (CTS Publications, 2004; Do 713).
Eucharist (CTS Publications, 2004; Do 714).
Reconciliation (CTS Publications, 2004; Do 716).
Anointing (CTS Publications, 2004; Do 711).
Marriage (CTS Publications, 2004; Do 710).
Holy Orders (CTS Publications, 2004; Do 715).

Informative Catholic Reading

We hope that you have enjoyed reading this booklet.

If you would like to find out more about CTS booklets - we'll send you our free information pack and catalogue.

Please send us your details:

Name ....

Address ....

....

....

Postcode ....

Telephone...

Email ....

Send to: CTS, 40-46 Harleyford Road,
            Vauxhall, London
            SE11 5AY

Tel: 020 7640 0042
Fax: 020 7640 0046
Email: info@cts-online.org.uk